BORN
TO BE
AWKWARD

ALSO BY MIKE BENDER AND DOUG CHERNACK

Awkward Family Photos

Awkward Family Pet Photos

Awkward Family Holiday Photos

Celebrating Those
Imperfect Moments of
Babyhood

born to be awkward

Mike Bender & Doug Chernack

 THREE RIVERS PRESS • NEW YORK

Published in the United States by Three Rivers Press,
an imprint of the Crown Publishing Group,
a division of Penguin Random House LLC, New York.
www.crownpublishing.com

Three Rivers Press and the Tugboat design are
registered trademarks of Penguin Random House LLC.

Library of Congress Cataloging-in-Publication Data
Bender, Mike, 1975–
  Born to be awkward: celebrating those imperfect moments
of babyhood / Mike Bender, Doug Chernack.
    pages cm
1. Infants—Humor. 2. Infants—Portraits. I. Chernack, Doug. II. Title.
 PN6231.I5B47 2015
 818'.602—dc23   2015014964

ISBN 978-0-8041-4073-7
eBook ISBN 978-0-8041-4074-4

Printed in the United States of America

Cover design by Christopher Brand
Cover photograph by Aleister Perry

10 9 8 7 6 5 4 3 2 1

First Edition

For Kai, Soe, Ravi, and Violet

CONTENTS

INTRODUCTION

We take more photos during our children's first few years than at any other time in their lives. These little bundles of joy are so innocent and cuddly that we can't help but be overwhelmed by our love for them—so we feel the need to document their every waking moment. The problem is most babies aren't quite ready for prime time. In fact, they're too busy trying to control the muscles in their faces and keep themselves from drooling to actually pose for a picture. Despite that, there we are, shoving our lenses in their faces and proudly capturing their first awkward family photos.

As new parents ourselves, the baby photos that are submitted to us are always near and dear to our hearts. We can appreciate the parental instinct to record every odd moment and the often unphotogenic results. It reminds us that we're not alone with our potty-training struggles, sibling rivalries, and birthday parties that never go according to plan.

This book features the most popular baby pictures from awkwardfamilyphotos.com, never-before-seen photos, stories, and even a special section that gives you, the reader, the ability to be a part of the book. We want to thank all of the generous big and little babies who were brave enough to share their most uncomfortable early moments with the world. And to all of the future parents out there—we hope this book serves as a cautionary tale. Because if we can save just one baby from an awkward photo, then we've done our job.

Mike and Doug

awkwardfamilyphotos.com

1

SAY CHEESE!

*We may not
be able to smile
or control our
bodily functions,
but for some reason
Mom and Dad think
we're ready
for our close-ups.*

HEADSTRONG

≫

*They were just waiting for
the rest of her body to arrive.*

Lilypad

Hey, it beats powder.

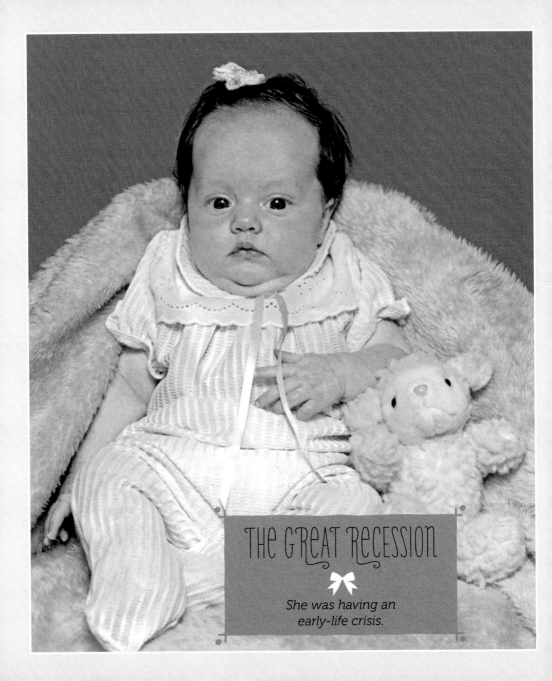

THE GREAT RECESSION

She was having an
early-life crisis.

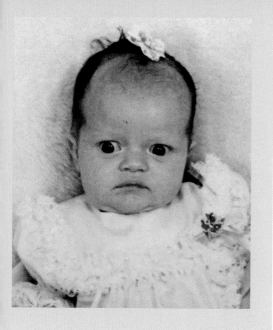

hair club for babies

Might as well
flaunt your forehead
while you're waiting
for your hair to grow in.

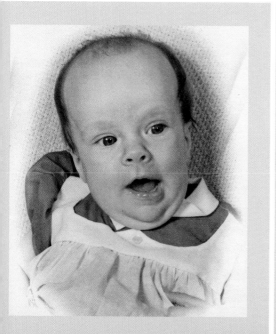

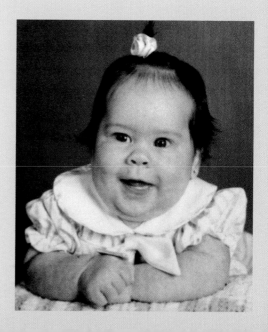

⇘ THE LAW OF DISTRACTION ⇙

Some plans were destined for failure.

The Daily Grind

Because nothing quite
captures the innocence of
childhood like being
photographed next to
a meat grinder.

PUT ON A HAPPY FACE

★

Just because they haven't mastered the smile
doesn't mean they can't light up a room.

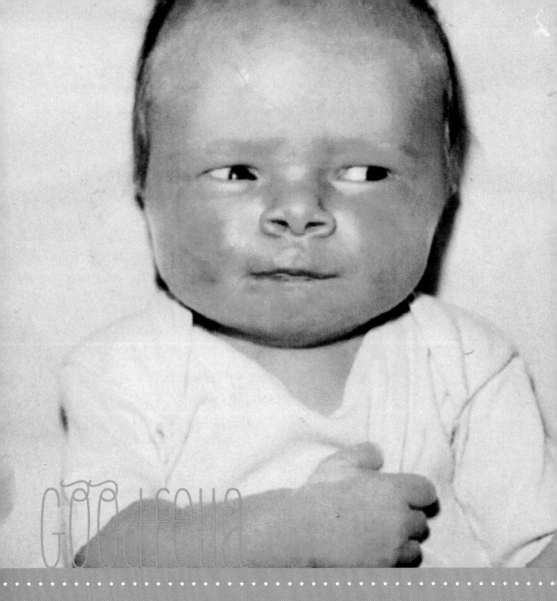

GOOdfella

Sometimes, you gotta rough a few people up.

the fall guy

The kid stays in the picture.

SWEATPROOF
The ladies approve.

MY FIRST BIKINI

It's never too early to rock a two-piece.

eyes wide open
You should see him when he's frightened.

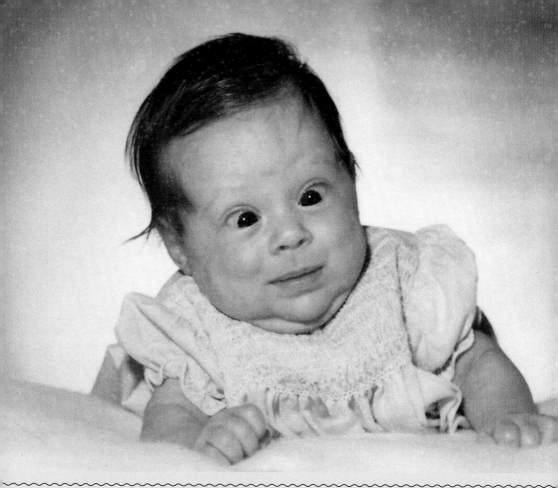

Focus

She needs everything to stay right where it is.

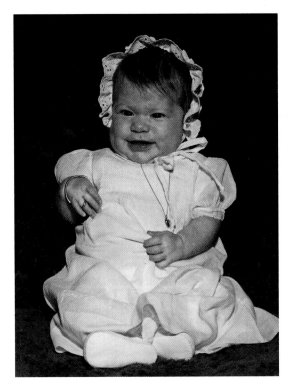

BEHIND THE AWKWARDNESS

My poor mother … not even a fancy gold
bracelet, ring, and locket can dress up the fact
that I was no beauty.

K.B.
Renton, Washington

Multiple Personalities

There are two sides
to every story.

FLIPPING OUT

She cannot tell a lie.

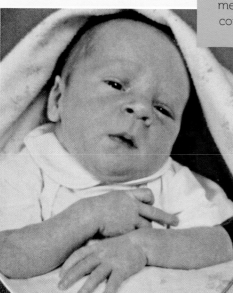

SIGN LANGUAGE

They can't talk yet, but that doesn't mean they aren't communicating.

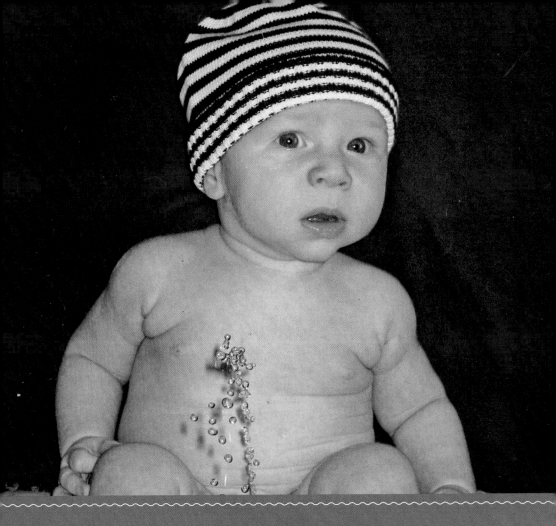

Ocean Spray

He just wants to find the leak.

SUPERPOWERS

~~~~~~~~~~~~

Little known fact:
all babies are born with
googly-ray vision.

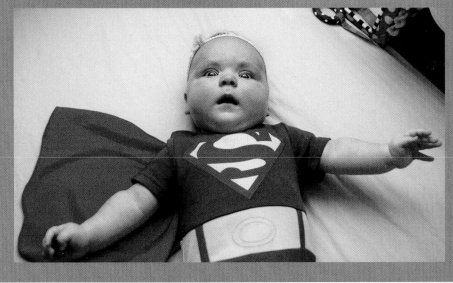

lean on me

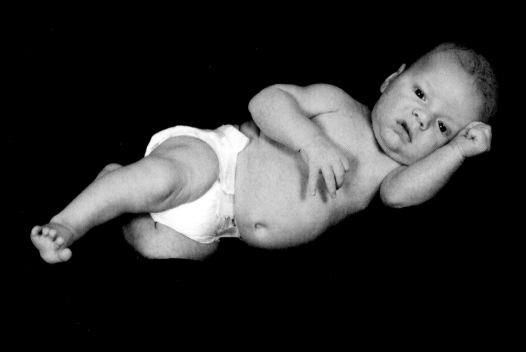

Go ahead. Make yourself uncomfortable.

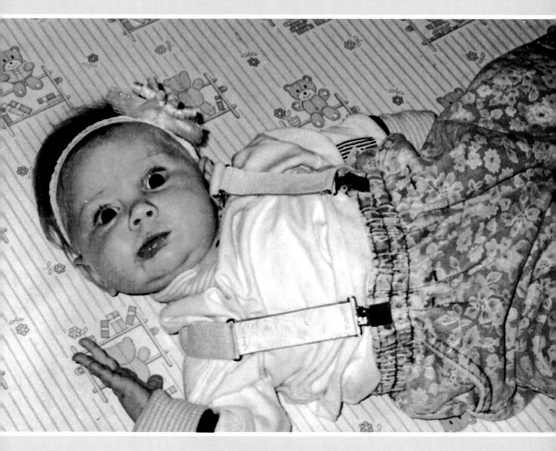

GET JIGGY WITH IT

She was choreographing her first break-dance routine.

SPIT-TAKE

Nothing complements a cute outfit
like a little drool, spit, snot, or throw-up.

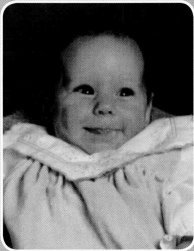

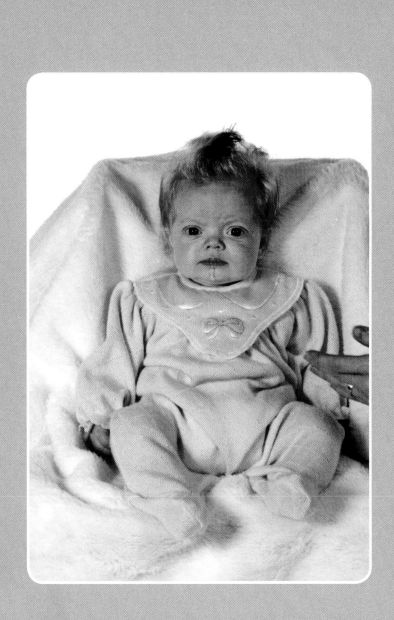

roll play

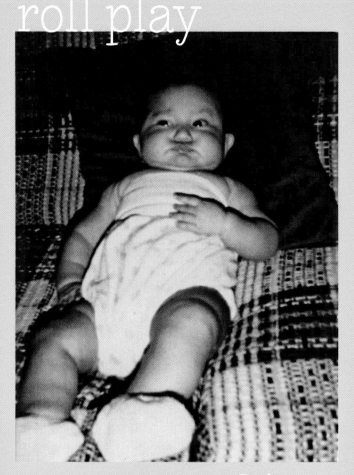

Don't get up.

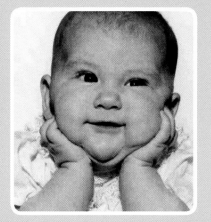

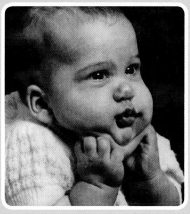

above the folds

With no neck muscles and several chins,
we can use the support.

SEE NO EVIL

According to him, this photo never happened.

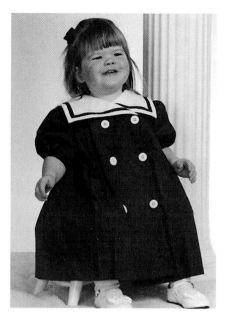

BEHIND THE AWKWARDNESS

This is me at the age of two. Many ludicrous things
have been said about this photo:

1. Are you hiding a small family underneath that dress?

2. Mom dressed me to look MUCH fatter than I was.

3. At least the rolls on my thighs are covered.

4. Were you training to be a sumo wrestler?

Molly
Murfreesboro, Tennessee

THE PARENT TRAP

*Everything we do,
we learn from
Mom and Dad.
The only problem is
they have no idea
what they're doing.*

HEADRESTS

Ah, the advantages of twins.

BEHIND THE AWKWARDNESS

We had just finished up a family reunion in California and decided to take some family pictures on the final day. Both kids were crying and we were pulling our hair out trying to get one good picture. Someone had the idea to do a candid photo of us swinging our kids. As we wound up for the final shot, I noticed something out of the corner of my eye, and I saw my son gracefully do a full backwards layout and land flat on his back in the sand. After about two minutes of sniffling, he was back to his regular self, smiling and laughing.

Steven
Castle Rock, Colorado

The Kids' Table

Hey, it was the '60s.

House Doctor

That's one way to take
his temperature.

TOP OF THE POPS

Special effects by Dad.

TUNE IN TOKYO

There is absolutely nothing useful about Dad's nipples,
which is what makes them so damn interesting.

KISSY FACE

Regrets, he's had a few.

THE IN-BETWEENERS
"Oh, don't mind me."

Fishy

HE WAS STILL DECIDING WHICH ONE TO THROW BACK.

THRILL OF THE HUNT

Dad showing off his prize catch.

MULLETING IT OVER

She just realized this
is her stylist.

Supercuts

Who needs a barber
when you've got the
steady and sure
hands of Mom?

The Squinch

You can see the resemblance.

THE MISSING PIECE

He promised he would keep an eye on her.

THE PAJAMA GAME

The original BabyBjörn.

A HELPING HAND

No wonder he preferred to be held by Mom.

BEHIND THE AWKWARDNESS

We were on vacation in Virginia visiting my aunt. My mom
and dad thought it'd be a good idea to get a picture of my brother and
me with the ocean in the background. And an even better idea to let
my brother hold the baby (me). Well, when my dad said "on the count
of three," my brother Matt thought he had to let go. My mom and
aunt caught my foot just in time. My dad kept snapping
the picture, which resulted in this family classic.

Heather
Saint Albans, Vermont

DADDY DAY CARE

What could possibly go wrong?

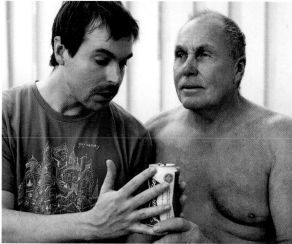

OLDER & WISER

Where do you think Mom &
Dad got their skills from?

BEHIND THE AWKWARDNESS

Leighton and I had been holding hands.
The photographer captured the perfect moment as she
leaned away from me. So, the rest of us are looking fabulous
while my two-year-old is crashing to the pavement.
Oh, and she fell again.

Ashley
McKinney, Texas

NEW KID ON THE BLOCK

Everyone is so excited

to meet the new baby . . .

that is, except for

our siblings.

{ first impressions }
Perhaps they were introduced a little too early.

Brotherly Love

Welcome to the neighborhood, kid.

BROTHERHEAD

As far as she was concerned, it just gave her a bigger target.

Centerpiece

All the scrutiny was making her uncomfortable.

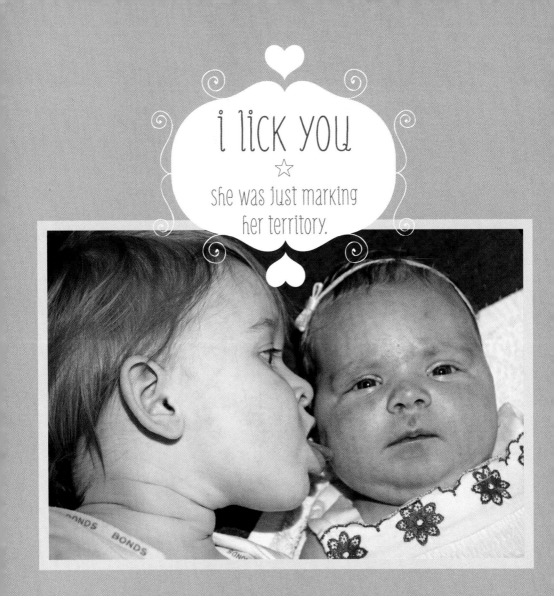

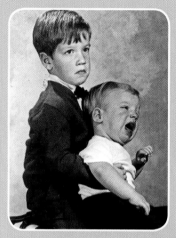

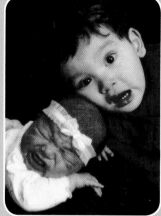

POKER FACES

Our brothers and
sisters can barely
contain their
excitement.

stuck on them

Duct tape really does work for everything.

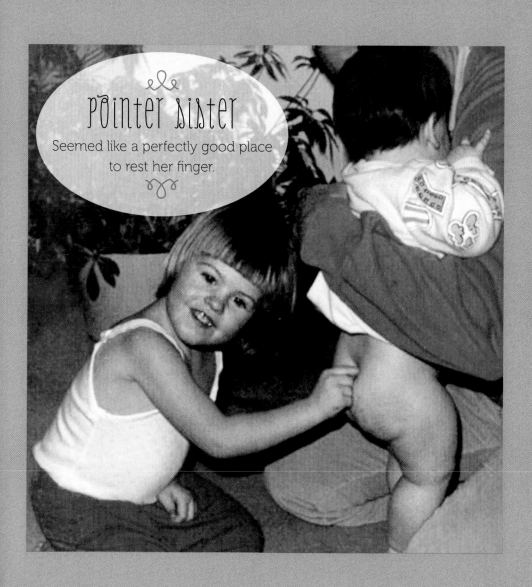

Pointer Sister

Seemed like a perfectly good place to rest her finger.

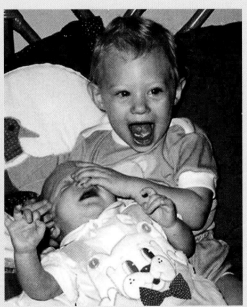

Face-Off

There are many ways
for our siblings to express
their affection, but there's
nothing quite as good as an
old-fashioned face-claw.

SNOWED IN

A premature hand-me-down.

ignore us doing this

spreading the love.

ALL
IN THE
FAMILY

Hey, at least
we have each other.

RE-CREATING
THE AWKWARDNESS

head under heels

sometimes, you just have to roll with it.

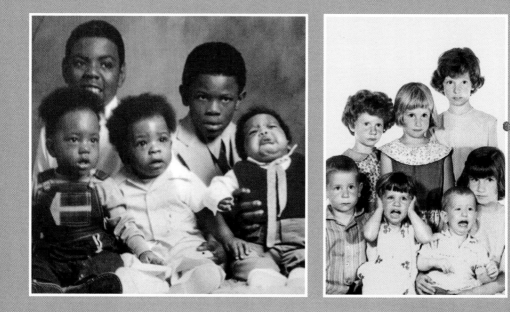

CRYBABIES

❦

It's no wonder our siblings want to send us back.

the usual suspect

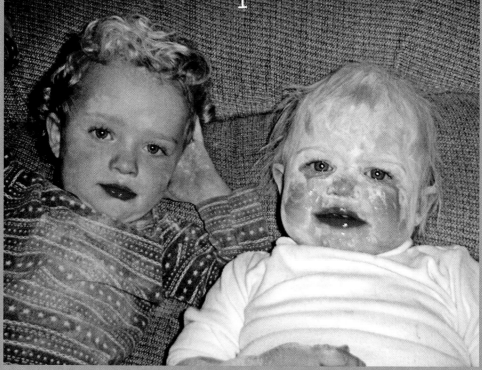

Just because you're cleaner doesn't mean you're innocent.

BEHIND THE AWKWARDNESS

I have no idea why I am holding a knife or have
a grenade strapped to my waist, but since I'm crying,
I can pretty much guarantee my older brother had
something to do with it.

Mary
Woodbridge, New Jersey

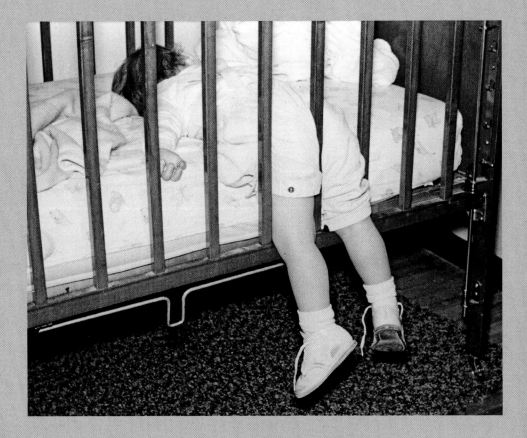

4

EAT, SLEEP, PLAY, POOP

These four simple activities

define our lives as babies . . .

unfortunately for our parents,

we haven't mastered any

of them yet.

DIAPER NINJA

Deadly, but far
from silent.

sleep training

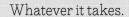

Whatever it takes.

GUESS WHO'S COMING
TO DINNER

❧

If you can't eat with them, join them.

PSI
He was framed.

Lipstick Jungle

Too much?

napkin, please

It's a short distance from table to
mouth, but so much can happen
along the way.

RE-CREATING
THE AWKWARDNESS

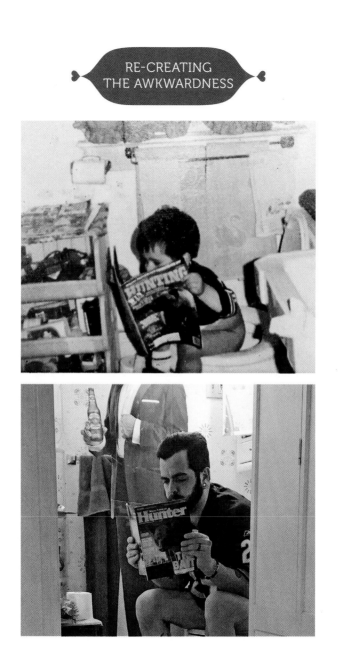

PEP TALK

It was their pre-game ritual.

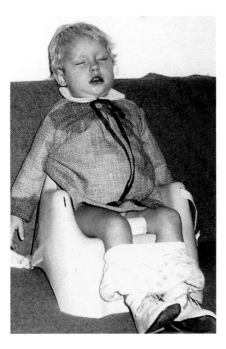

BEHIND THE AWKWARDNESS

It was my first birthday, and apparently, I had
licked all of my parents' friends' liquor glasses empty.
After returning, Mom saw me falling
backward and passing out. The medics called
to the scene made me vomit and sat me on the throne.
Sadly, nothing much has changed.

Beatrice
Tsim Sha Tsui, Hong Kong

BABY'S DAY OUT

Getting out of the house was
exactly what she needed.

BUN IN THE...

~~~~~~~~~~

Everything is a toy
when you're a baby.

IN YOUR GRILL

it was his walden pond.

Taking the Plunge

❧

His search for answers had begun.

Fabric Softener

She preferred the gentle cycle.

SLEEPYHEADS

♥

Who needs a crib when there are so many comfortable places to catch some z's?

BEHIND THE AWKWARDNESS

At the time of this photo, my family lived in a small town
off a busy highway. My little sister was a wanderer and had a
tendency to put everything in her mouth. We needed a solution to
keep her in sight and out of trouble—the only thing we had was
baling twine, which we kept tied to the gutter.

Cindy
Lake Stevens, Washington

BEHIND THE AWKWARDNESS

Remember those plastic easels that we had as kids?
One day while I was visiting my grandparents, my marker
fell underneath mine, and while I was looking for it, the
easel collapsed on top of me. My "concerned" parents decided
to wait a bit to see if I could free myself. Mom is taking
the picture, and Dad can barely be seen on the left.

Mitch
Austin, Texas

blame it on the rain

That was enough sensory exploration for the moment.

BLADES OF GLORY
It was like watching the grass grow.

Potty Party

Some kids need a support group.

Water Fountain

Oh, like *you've* never wanted to.

splish splash

If it looks like a bath and
feels like a bath . . .

5

LET THE GOOD TIMES ROLL

We learn from a very early age that no matter the holiday or special occasion, we are destined to be miserable.

bah, humbug!
Never lick a gift horse in the mouth.

mellow yellow

And thus began her distrust of furries.

OUR
LITTLE PUMPKIN
He had found his costume.

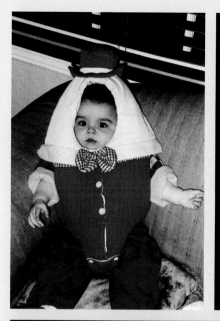

COSTUME PARTY

when we're babies,
our parents get to
choose our costumes,
and clearly, they can't
be trusted.

Stuck on Them

This cupid had a range of six inches.

Rudy

This reindeer didn't make the weigh-in.

SILLY RABBITS
Somewhere, there is an aunt responsible for this.

head games

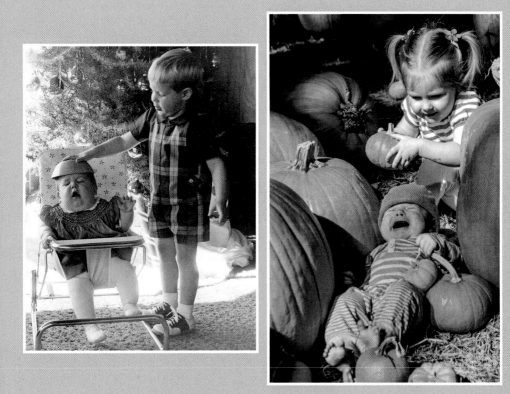

we can always count on our brother and sister
to pass on the holiday spirit.

ONE IS THE LONELIEST
It's her party and she can
cry if she wants to.

TERRIFYING TWOS
It's her party and everyone
should be afraid. Very afraid.

BEHIND THE AWKWARDNESS

I'm the baby, and this was my first Halloween.
I guess it shut me up when they put a finger in my mouth,
so my grandma thought it would be funny if she put
her finger in my dad's mouth to shut him up.
And my great-grandma followed suit.

Spencer
Evanston, Illinois

crappy birthday

Every king
deserves a throne.

nightmare on elm street

That'll teach her to ask for another doll.

STRANGER DANGER

We teach our kids not to talk to strangers, but it's totally cool to sit on the lap of a freakish holiday mascot.

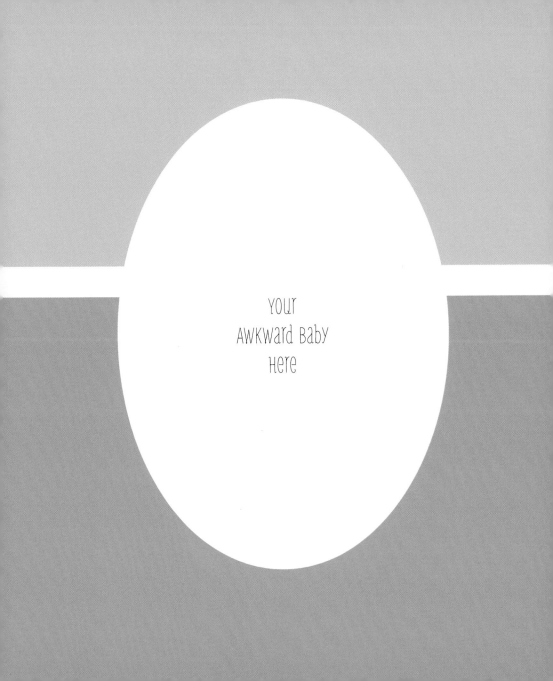

your
AWKWard BaBY
Here

MY AWKWARD BABY

This is an opportunity to celebrate the awkward photos of your own child. C'mon, we know you've got them.

Nailed it.

And this was a *good* hair day.

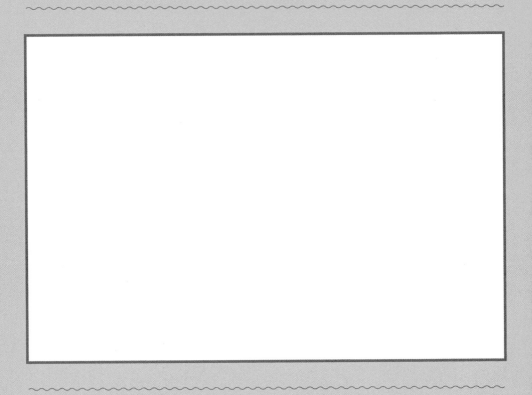

PEOPLE TELL ME THIS
IS MY BEST ANGLE.

DOES this make me look fat?

Messy is the new black.

FYI, THESE ARE NOT TEARS OF JOY.

These should go viral.

Don't hate me
because I'm
beautiful.

ACKNOWLEDGMENTS

WE WOULD LIKE TO THANK: All of the families who have so generously shared their awkward baby photos with us and the always enthusiastic team at Three Rivers Press, including our superstar editor, Suzanne O'Neill (who has witnessed our transformations from two boring guys to two boring dads), Jenni Zellner, Julie Cepler, Gianna Antolos, Ellen Folan, Matthew Martin, Elizabeth Rendfleisch, Tricia Boczkowski, Jacob Lewis, and Molly Stern.

MIKE BENDER WOULD LIKE TO THANK: My wife, SuChin, not just for tolerating this strange career path I've taken, but for being an amazing sounding board all of these years. My son, Kai, and my daughter, Soe (page 98)—you are the lights of my life and I look forward to every single day I get to spend with you. You make me so proud and constantly remind me of what's truly important. I only hope that when you grow up, you will look back and understand what the hell Daddy was doing all these years. To the rest of my family and friends, whose unwavering support for a guy who posts wacky photos every day means more to me than you'll ever know. And finally, to Kenny and Selma Furst—while they may not be here in person to celebrate this book, I will never forget the standing ovation they received at our first book signing in New York City. Their spirit and their humor will live on in everything we do at AFP, and I love them very much.

DOUG CHERNACK WOULD LIKE TO THANK: My wife, Amy, for all her love and support. My family, for their love, their encouragement, and for still not fully understanding what an actual awkward family photo is, which has led to so many great submissions. My friends, for always showing up for us—you've saved us from many nights of empty rooms and awkward silences. And, of course, my children, Ravi and Violet, for reminding me on a daily basis of how lucky I am and to whom I wholeheartedly apologize in advance for bringing into the family business (page 98, in case anyone is interested).

PHOTO CREDITS

Page 10: Michelle McCleary; page 12: Karl Klemmick; page 13: Isabella Kirk; page 14: Bradley Hughes; page 15: Nadia Watson (*top left*), Diane Kinsel (*bottom left*), #throwbackthursdayallison (*bottom right*); page 16: the Culver Family; page 17: Rachel Zirkin Duda; page 18: Kerry Carmack Brinkman (*top*), Ida Stodell (*bottom left*), anonymous (*bottom right*); page 19: anonymous (*top*), Amanda Turner—J. Berger Photography (bottom); page 20: Janna Baty; page 21: Minda Dwyer; page 22: anonymous; page 23: Rachel M. (*left*), Knoll Larkin (*right*); page 24: the Feasel Family; page 25: anonymous; page 26: K.B. VanHorn; page 27: Vanessa Almonte; page 28: Cary Maish Brodie; page 29: Mike Buettner (*top left*), Aden Joseph Hutchins (*top right*), Nathaniel Honka (*bottom left*), Ghita Giammalvo (*bottom right*); page 30: Basma (*left*), Dee Eva (*right*); page 31: Ginger A. Plumbo; page 32: anonymous; page 33: Greg Taylor Tanis (*top*), Michelle McCleary (*bottom*); page 34: Tiffany S.; page 35: Michelle Hess; page 36: the Tierney Family (*top left*), anonymous (*top right*), the Braun Family (*bottom left*), anonymous (*bottom right*); page 37: anonymous; page 38: Shianne Allen; page 39: Alice Wernimont Bodnar (*top left*); Laura Hunter (*top right*), Joe Costa (*bottom*); page 40: Angela Webb; page 41: anonymous; page 42: Guylaine Meeks and Darrell Meeks; page 44: Sienna, Elihu, and Ezra Herrin; page 45: Steven Cramer; page 46: the Sheahan Family; page 47: Matthew Volpe; page 48: Carlos Aguayo; page 49: Herbert Schmon (*left*), anonymous (*right*); page 50: Jackson and Daddy; page 51: the Birdsall Family (*top left*), the Beery Family (*top right*); Shelita Thomas, Reginald Thomas, and Sheroid Thomas (*bottom*); page 52: Pete Shea; page 53: the Green Family; page 54: Erika Lambert; page 55: Wendi Davis Ottoson, Linda Davis, William Davis, Staci Davis Ratkovich, Jodi Davis Hickey (*top right*), anonymous (*bottom left*); Janice (*bottom right*); page 56: Margaret and Baby Clark; page 57: the Shawcroft Family; page 58: the Kuzara Family; page 59: the McCormicks; page 60: Heather Tynon; page 61: Brandi Serrano and Richard Serrano (*top*), Leah Renee Peterson (*bottom left*), the George Family (*bottom right*); page 62: the Walton Family; page 63: Gary Budjinski (both); page 64: Michelle Brown (*top*), Shelley Gaylor (*bottom*); page 65: the Hardcast Family (both); page 66: Eleanor May; page 68: Lisa Pratt; page 69: Scott Kradolfer; page 70: Tim Howard; page 71: Brittany; page 72: Michelle McCleary; page 73: Kenneth Olsen (*top left*), Dev L. Swann (*top center*), Derek Mayo (*top right*), Curtis Jones (*bottom*); page 74: Gavin Grounds; page 75: Kristen Rowe; page 76: T.W. Lawrence; page 77: anonymous; page 78: Alisha Abner (*top left*), Jennifer M. Burnett (*top right*), Stacey Zynen (*bottom*); page 79: anonymous; page 80: Kelly Lavan; page 81: Helen Buck Chatman, Ruthanne Buck, and Jane Buck; page 82: Danielle Davis; page 83: Julie Taylor (*top left*), David Hines (*top right*), Julian and Anne Hebert (*bottom*); page 84: Jerry Jobe (*both*); page 85: Cory Gilstrap; page 86: the Kirby Boys (*top left*), Lucy Descalso Reynolds (*top right*), Elizabeth Fink (*bottom left*), Johanna Brown (*bottom right*); page

87: Amber Meyers; page 88: Justin Hill; page 89: Marcy S.; page 90: Alice Wernimont Bodnar; page 93: Melissa Straw and Shauna Straw; page 94: Erin Singleton; page 95: Tracy R. and R. Hughes; page 96: Kacie Kuehn; page 97: anonymous (top), anonymous (center), Deniece Rudd (bottom); page 98: Doug Chernack (top left), Mike Bender (top right), Mike Bender (bottom left), Doug Chernack (bottom right); page 99: Scott Janes (both); page 100: Jerry Glassman; page 101: Beatrice Walter; page 102: Rachel Wachstein; page 103: the Hetherington Family (top), April A. Lillis (bottom); page 104: Melanie G.; page 105: Marlowe Hartnett; page 106: Annette Stapleton Heywood; page 107: Aaron Battle (top left), Jones-Doran Family (top right), Anna Sparkman (bottom); page 108: Melissa Wygand (top left), anonymous (top right), Kathy Romeo (bottom); page 109: Lapter Family; page 110: Cindy K. Sween; page 111: Mitch Metcalfe; page 112: Jim Lowe; page 113: Patricia L.; page 114: Robert Brokamp; page 115: Steven; page 116: Ben Smith; page 117: Bradley Smith (top), Max (bottom); page 118: Ashley J. Larson; page 120: Julie and Amelia Arnold; page 121: Shawna Quinn and Kyle Manske (both); page 122: Allie Mackay; page 123: the McKinlay Family; page 124: Mike, Danyel, and T; page 125: Liz Zargoza (top left), Julie Arnold, Lovenote Creative, LLC, South Milwaukee, WI (top right), anonymous (bottom); page 126: Anna Thron; page 127: the Durbin Family; page 128: the Bosserman Family; page 129: Angela Follett Nolan (left), Frank Hostler (right); page 130: Meghann, Katie, and Ben; page 131: Tamara Kronk; page 132: Spencer James Parks; page 133: anonymous; page 134: Cathy Ovsak and Jordan Tucker; page 135: Rachel Meserve (top left), Sarah Beri (top right), Melani H. Bigger (bottom left); page 136: Tim Duff (top left), Natalie Pozo (top right), anonymous (bottom left), the Hunt and Fritz Family (bottom right); page 137: Claire and Jon; page 149 (collage, in alphabetical order): Hannah Abrams; Alicia; Jessie Allred; April; Becky Bailey; Carol (Hauth) Barker; Danny Ray Barnes; Rachael Baumgartner; Kelly Bennett; the Bilodeau Family; Michelle Bredehoft; Sarah the Bunny; Jordan Burk; Nancy Burton and Annie Leue; Cooper Campbell; Stacey Campbell; the Chiles Family; Claire, Andrew, and Michelle; Tim Clemens; the Clarke Boys; Dan Cummings; the Daussat Family; the Doyle Family; Teals Dryden; Allison Duncan-Holland; Jennifer Encarnación; the Ewing Family; the Gallivan Family; the Galvin Family; Sarah Garrison; Gregory-Fords; Bryan Grubb; Damon and Lee (Scooter) Guyett; Kelly Holmes; the Holohan Family; Dashiell Bark-Huss; Jennifer Ives; Teddy Iten-Scott; Jeff and Tina; Della Gould Jordan; Renee Celine Junot; the Kenny Family; Kaisha Kristensen; the Kucharski Boys; Sarah Lapp; the Lee Family; Kristen Lefler; Jim and Renee Lemakos; Lori; Vanessa Rojas Luna; Barbara Mackinson; Marlene; Mary; Nicholas Masse; the Maxwell Family; Makenna Miner; Megan; Brandon Moats; Debi Moravetz; the Morgan Family; Eva Mullen; the Nusom Family; Jordan O'Brien; the O'Donnell Family; Emilie Oliva; Amy and Stephanie Owens; Katherine Palmer; the Payne Family; Jerimiah Penland; the Perry Twins; the Peterson Family of Michigan; Jenn Preston; Jillian Quail; Rachel and Aisling; Ed Raleigh; Bjorn K. Ranheim; Kristen Haas-Reckelhoff; Sara Reidy; the Rush Family; Kristin S.; the Sanders Family; Megann M. Schmidt; the Selgrath Family; Wahid Shafique; Shauna—Michigan; Sylvia Kiser and Conner Smith; the Southerland Family; Melody Stallings-Mann; Summer Steele; Wendy Megan Stewart; Harit Stigson; Chris Summers; Lincoln "Loves His Mama" Swineford and Sean R. Swineford; Cindy Taulu; the Tiberg; Pawl Tisdale; Connor Trost; Darla R. Turner; Adrianne VanDreumel; Michelle Vice; the Walker Family; Jayme Washburn; Stephanie West; Jennalee Williams; Charity Woodrum; Elizabeth Y.; Sophie Yates; Qing Zhao

ABOUT THE AUTHORS

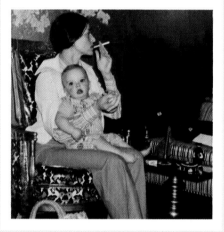

MIKE

"My mother's going to kill me, but here she is sharing some second-hand smoke with me as a baby. For the record, this might be the only cigarette she ever smoked."

DOUG

"Shortly after this picture was taken, my diaper exploded and leaked through my OshKosh B'goshes."